T0145290

Switchgrass

Poems
about marriage, illness, and the healing power
of love and nature

MARIE KANE

AuthorHouse™
1663 Liberty Drive
Bloomington, IN 47403
www.authorhouse.com
Phone: 833-262-8899

Because of the dynamic nature of the Internet, any web addresses or links contained in this book may have changed
since publication and may no longer be valid. The views expressed in this work are solely those of the author and do
not necessarily reflect the views of the publisher, and the publisher hereby disclaims any responsibility for them.

Any people depicted in stock imagery provided by Getty Images are models,
and such images are being used for illustrative purposes only.
Certain stock imagery © Getty Images.

This book is printed on acid-free paper.

ISBN: 978-1-7283-7767-4 (sc)
ISBN: 978-1-7283-7766-7 (e)

Library of Congress Control Number: 2023901216

Print information available on the last page.

Published by AuthorHouse 04/21/2023

authorHOUSE®

When it is dark enough,
you can see the stars.

~ Ralph Waldo Emerson (1803-1882)

Dedication

Switchgrass is dedicated to the late Christopher Bursk, extraordinary poet, teacher of poetry, mentor and friend, whose encouragement of and enthusiasm for this collection helped bring it to fruition

&

to all of the Kitchen Table poets, especially Wendy Steginsky, Monica Flint, Alan Toltzis, Lynda Gene Rymond, and Lavinia Kumar whose close revision of many of this book's poems helped tremendously, thanks to Alan Chazaro of *Black Lawrence Press* for his editing expertise, many thanks to Steve Nolan for his intelligent and careful editing, to Cheryl Baldi, whose book, *The Shapelessness of Water* showed me the way, to the staff at AuthorHouse for their close attention to this manuscript

&

to our children and grandchildren whose love reminds us what matters and is possible

&

above all, to my wonderful husband, Stephen Millner, whose loving care enables me to live and write.

&

as always, to my dear mom, Jean, and talented brother, Marty—
forever the cheerleaders.

Statement by Wendy Fulton Steginsky

I have known Marie Kane for almost twenty years. Our paths have crossed and continue to at area poetry venues and workshops: at poetry salons and events held at the Writers Room in Doylestown, PA where I worked until its closure in 2005; at Dr. Christopher Bursk's Master Class at Bucks County Community College where I attended for seventeen years until he died in 2021; at Marie's Kitchen Table poetry workshop which she has run every other week since 2009.

Marie and I co-edited an anthology of poetry, *Carry Us to the Next Well* (Kelsay Books, 2021) to honor the tenth anniversary of Kitchen Table poetry and a dear poet friend who was an original member of that group and died tragically in 2018.

Again, in 2022, Marie and I and another poet, Lavinia Kumar, co-edited and published a poetry anthology, *A Certain Kind of Swagger* to honor the life and teachings of our mentor, Dr. Christopher Bursk.

I have had three books of my own poetry published by Kelsay Books: *The Tide of Bermuda's Light* in 2014, *Let This Be Enough*, 2016, and *Where River's Mouth Meets Ocean*, 2019. Marie and I are both very familiar with each other's work and I have a great respect and love for all her books, particularly her latest, *Switchgrass*.

Acknowledgements:

I am grateful for the following journals for publishing these poems,
some in a different form or title.

Delaware Valley Poetry Anthology	*"To Die Just That Much"*
The River	"What Rises?"
River Heron Review	"They Need to Dream Here"
Schuylkill Valley Journal	"Watercolor of the Winter Sea" "Mooncake Festival" "Learning the Roads of the Sea" *"In Every Life, Both"*
Wordgathering	"I Can Say Now That Things Are Not What They Seem"
U.S. 1 Worksheets	"On a Spring-fed New Hampshire Lake" "She's Radiant"
Kane, Marie, *Beauty, You Drive a Hard Bargain*. Utah: Kelsay Books, 2017. p. 96.	"For Love to Be Had"

Contents

Summertime Embraces Our Ten-Year-Old Selves

~ Every second is of infinite value. ~ Goethe

Sky unwraps morning, evening shuts day
down, calendar flips pages
month upon month, year upon year.
Let's slow time's progress,
discern time's wrinkle, revisit expansive July
when summertime embraces our ten-year-old
selves: forts, dams on streams,
pick-up baseball games, bikes, jacks, and leaning
against the candy store display
with pennies or a nickel hot in our hands
to buy Necco Wafers, Candy
Buttons, Tootsie Rolls—a moment away. We play
hide-and-seek after dinner 'till
light fades, 'til *Olly, olly, oxen free*
sounds out to a red and purple sunset.
Our names echo from sides of stucco houses, narrow
garages: *Marty, Marie, Julie, Maurice,*
Carolyn . . . . Porch lights trigger each child home.

Switchgrass Near the Delaware River

Spindle of catbird music tips
　　toward budding oak trees
　　　　that muffle swooping
crow's sharp notes and blue jay's
　　rusty-pump voice.
　　　　　　Spring Beauty's white-
pink and cornflower's bright
　　blue covet open spaces all
　　　　the way to the river
where celery-green switchgrass rises
　　eight feet topped by grass-
　　　　bunch-yellow—
brighter than the glassy sun.
　　Deep roots subdue flood,
　　　　control washout—
survive the inevitable.

His Hand Finds Hers

In the first heat of a long-ago
spring, they play tag on the river-

bank amidst green and silver-blue
switchgrass. Betrothed to the sky,

they silently thread in and out
of top-heavy stalks—even as new

foliage ambushes their faces,
shoulders. He waits. His hand

finds hers. She fingers his palm—
a fortune teller predicting their lavish

future. How comforting it is to be confident
in years to come—to know of no leg

failure, deadening fatigue, curled
left hand that cannot button, nor grasp.

Still

If she could dance—legs quick, arms fluid—
any dance would do. Salsa, square, twist, rumba,
or the intimate waltz shared years ago at their July

wedding when MS had not yet crooked its finger
for her, nor had amyloidosis taken his job and left
numbing pain, crippling fatigue, and the depression

that capped them off. His evenings spin around
a black hole and still he sways her when they can—
he, who can do so little for himself.

Lesions, Erosion, and Snakes

Brain lesions flash white on her MRI—nerve sheaths

erode like soft rock pounded by water. Her rock, *(not*

granite—hardened in fire then slowly cooled—)

but rock soft as soapstone and talc, renders her defenseless

against this maddening washing away of nerve

sheaths, while His body hosts garden snakes   that deposit

protein mayhem in each organ — shutting down working

parts at will. Yet his disease disappears when medicine's

spade lifts to strike. What if his garden snakes

become coiled rattlers that flick their forked tongues

without tasting fear at medicine's presence?

Why Are They Not Yet Desperate?

She wonders—if water's assault
    erodes everything, how will
she recognize the way to him?

He wonders—if coiling snakes
    block all paths, how will
he find any to her?

They both wonder why they are not
    yet desperate, and what will
happen if they become so?

 Shaman

~after Octavio Paz

Wet your dark hair darker,
    rinse your mouth
full with lake water's clarity—
    a wholeness of water
giving life.

Step forward—accept
    lake's force,
grasp lake's light, sing
    your name to bass
and crayfish, to underwater
    granite and cold-water
springs—shaman to illness,
    shaman to fears.

Visualize rebirth—between
    what is seen
and what is felt,
    between what is felt
and what is surmised,
    between what
is surmised and what is
    known.

The lake begins as a spring-
    filled, glacier-carved
bowl and becomes
    your life force.

On a Spring-fed New Hampshire Lake

Wind scallops lake water into troughs and ridges
　　that move in concert as if tightened by
a drawstring from the shore then released.
　　Lake's blue-white surface becomes sky's

white-blue mirror. She watches him on the wooden
　　dock—he settles to soak in summer's untamed
light that pins him at noon to his recliner. But she
　　needs something to eat—and medicine.

Why didn't he bring her lunch when she asked?
　　She sighs, thinks, *How can she complain*?
Yet she does. Shifting her weight, she yells, *I need
　　lunch and my meds. I asked already!*

No response. High over the lake in a widespread,
　　noisy flock, birds echo her complaint with loud
cries. A motorboat trailing a skier sends plumes
　　of water his way. Her frustrations surface

as loons do on the lake—popping up unexpectedly.
　　Can she ignore the backdrop of illness,
of disability, willing them to diminish? She could
　　wear the blue sky, bend with the slight bow

and rise of silver birch trees whose fallen leaves under-
    neath are confetti compressed. Between trees'
rustling, sun pours through and places its hot, white stamp
    on the path to the dock. Struggling, he gets up,

heads to the kitchen, brings her back a sandwich
    with leafy lettuce showing. What a physically-
challenged pair—*perishable,* as it says on the lettuce
    container. He helps her skirt sun's focused laser

to sit under the red pine in her most supportable chair,
    where she opts for resilience, its own kind of shade.

Before Summer Sun Owns the Lake

She is charted, marked—her exhilaration
    straitjacketed—she groans with this
morning's attempt to rise. His wide hands
    reach her narrow ones and he pulls
her forward till she sits on the side of the bed.

He speaks of their canoe trip later that morning
    before summer sun owns the lake.
He straps on her left leg brace, helps her dress,
    serves tart blueberry pancakes
on the screened porch. She navigates

the cleared path to the dock with her walker.
    Life jacket secured, she leans over
the clear lake; he stands next to his father's
    green canoe, catches her, then lifts
her into the padded seat.

His arms, strong—his face, strained.
    The lake spreads a table dressed
in cobalt cloth. He paddles to their backwater
    bay to greet dense summer switchgrass
and waxy lilies that float like golden Fiestaware.

In Every Life, Both

~Louise Glück

Moon's tail of light touches
the lake's calm water and secluded
shore toward Pegasus and a broad
line of distant trees.

Across the water, lights of homes
wink on. A passing boat sounds
its two powers: presence and sorrow.
In every life, both.

A stripe of cloud forms under
the almost-full moon. The loon's
nest on Spectacle Island cocoons
its eggs amid dense grass and weeds,

while one long loon call wavers over
darkening water, the reply—distant,
trailing—stills the heart.
He says, *look at those clouds holding*

up the moon, that light, that reflection,
the boat moving and breaking up the lake.
The boat passes, and the wavering path
of silver light opens, then closes. Still,

there is no wind. I take the chance
this offers, absorb the boat's caution
and the loon's comfort, rise from my chair,
one hand clutching my cane, the other

the top railing post, then letting go to turn
and receive his offer of brandy, auburn
    liquid
gleaming in the transfer. *Some of us*
    make our
own light, he says—toasting the still moon

and we two—*here's to us, and this light.*

Lucknow

A millennium ago, New Hampshire volcano rose ten
thousand feet until its fiery insides erupted propelling orange
magma, massive rocks, pumice into the sky. Quick flowing lava

created imposing granite formations that coated the forest
for miles. The flattened Ossipee mountain's interior lay exposed—
a perfect oval, a hollow caldera. Near one volcanic outcrop stands

Lucknow—the mansion where stained glass windows cheer the cool
granite stones of its construction. Turrets' staircase walls—smooth
rocks tumbled by Merrimack's turbulent river—lead to views

of the lake at each spiral's turn. Outside, he and she chance fate
on an outcrop's thin volcanic edge. They lean, admire the island-
sprinkled lake far below bound by pitch and loblolly pines and swear

they can follow the narrow thread of the tarred road that leads
to their cabin.

They Dream the Same Fragmented Dream

When the power flickers out at their rented
cabin with a view of *Lucknow*'s tiled roof,

candles are no match for lightening that brings
their pine-paneled bedroom into sudden view

as if a vintage camera had *whooshed* alive every
few seconds. When the storm migrates south

from Moultonborough to Laconia, they dream
the same fragmented dream:

snowy heads of Queen Anne's lace tumble
over a row of rusty mailboxes leaning

to the right . . . lake buries granite boulders
the size of cars . . . water's edge teems

with ducks, their sharp beaks compete
with fingers plucking blueberries,

vivid green switchgrass frames their
backwater bay— that unruffled bit of water . . . .

The storm, candles, dream:
summer's end.

Each Late Afternoon

Autumn: They need each one, each first light's
                      golden aster to last into the next
         fresh morning, and each late afternoon
                      to offer a view of burgundy switch-
         grass with its tumultuous cascade. Fall floats
                      across his or her vision like migrating
         geese. He insists the season's shortened
                      dusk enables more time for moonlight
         and stars to share the sky.

River Walk

Perhaps it is as he says—

*(As wood smoke trails over
stubbled fields near trees'
architecture where leaves*

*gather on soon-to-be frosted
ground, where in the leafless
sugar maple a squirrel's nest*

*of thin twigs and leaves rests
in the twilight, almost floating
on air—till the sun lowers*

*itself below the hazy horizon—
chill predicting winter's approach—
it is then our arms fold 'round*

*each other, waist and hips
held, as we watch night crown
the horizon—.)*

"Our time together is infinite."

Mooncake Festival

A flock of geese obeys the rule of moon's fall light,
    cries their goodbyes above copper trees,

and disappears into purpling sky that runs to the other
    side of the universe. Over the river, harvest moon

illuminates the last stragglers. In her moon dreams,
    symmetry and balance rule her legs,

yet when awake, she staggers, falls, while any hope
    of recovery skitters into the moon's reflection

and river's depth. How to rout the burdens that threaten
    to capsize her? She knows of a Mooncake

Festival in the Far East where families send lanterns
    to the full moon carrying promising messages

to loved ones—living or the ancients—in the belief
    that they, too, are sending hopeful letters

to the same moon. Would the moon release one of their
    lanterns so that it drifts as an autumn leaf toward

her outstretched hands? She'd pluck the note from
    the air, unfold the envelope, relish the moon-wish

within. Tonight's obstinate moon sends no floating lantern.
    How foolish to wait again tomorrow, yet she will.

She accounts for tenth-month constellations—Perseus,
    Pegasus, and Taurus the Bull—tightens the woolen

scarf around her shoulders, and with the moon as witness,
    calls to her husband for a push home.

Learning the Roads of the Sea

Wild sea rakes sand out in fall storms—
      but do not give up the grit
      within that sounds your depth
and builds the unexpected.

Do not lose sight of distant lights
      on stormy seas—rising
      and falling spirits, cresting
and dropping—they may yet save you.

Rilke says, *all is known to you*—
      the wildness of open
      ocean, or the sandy, switch-
grass edge of the bay's polished surface.

Create sandcastles on the beach (soon
      to be ocean-absorbed),
      but first, bejewel their walls
with purple and blue sea glass so when

you knock, they let you in to cross
      the splendid threshold—
      undulating, gills forming—
learning the roads of the sea.

I Can Say Now That Things Are Not What They Seem

~ After Mark Strand, "Velocity Meadows"

Standing on the porch and hearing your shovel
move early snow to the rocky side of the driveway,
I feel December's cold flicker like a tossed mane.
Moon's light reveals our slanted snowfield;
a distant train's drawn-out call drifts
over early winter. Wind spins *a frieze
of clouds* that briefly close the light.

You interrupt your labor to watch me
test my quad cane on the snowy step.
Our neighbor's muted lamppost tempts
me across driveway's icy chasm.
What comfort is there when life puckers
its lips as if to kiss, then steals away, taunting?
I step off the porch into snow's white lines
that sift, revise the world.
An owl cries from snow-tinged trees
out back. Slim starlight gathers
at the gray fence line.

Your windswept warnings.
My precarious footfalls on fresh snow.

This Outside Peril

Who visits the rough Atlantic Ocean in the twelfth
     month? It pulls and thunders, rears back
and falls over itself, tugging sound over sand.

Their small house huddles the shoreline almost
     too close to water—a gusty nor'easter
could sweep it away.

Above heavy snowfall, winter switchgrass
     and its cinnamon seed-heads emerge—
erect, stalwart, alive.

We are heady at the threat of danger as if this
     outside peril eclipses the one inside of me,
the one inside of you.

Their New Year

Winter wind raises his blue and orange Delta
  as winder-line hums, spins through gloves,
    disappears into too-bright noon that

sunglasses barely dim. Steep thermals seize his kite
  singing toward sunlight. Forty, fifty, seventy-
    five yards of line unspool into stinging

sea wind. How can he stand, exposed to it all, his bright
  kite navigating fierce gusts? Last day at the sea
    house—he can stay at water's edge—

but she's inhaled enough of ocean's salt, absorbed lengthy
  silences between rowdy meetings of tide and sand.
    She needs to return to cabin's warmth—

remove gloves, hat, scarf—savor their yellow fireplace
  that soothes frozen hands, crooked limbs. She calls
    her daughter to bring her over the dune.

From windows, they watch his skillful hands work the wind,
  allow this wild kite to herald sky's expanse, grant sky's
    abandon, bless their New Year.

Watercolor of the Winter Shore

Palette, brushes, and brandy glass flank his
    watercolor of the winter shore. Snow
conceals the shore's sand, meets cold blue's
    long, slow waves, rounds the corners
of lifeguard stands. Snow appears colder under
    star light, warmer in shadows cast by
their dark house. Flat snow holds hints of purple,
    and in sleigh's gouge, snow reflects
silver-grey moonlight, a tugging charcoal base,
    its primal relationship to water.

Listen to the Wood Burn

Late winter launches from gray clouds—blizzard's downward
trajectory explodes. He carries blankets and his disabled
wife to the wrap-around porch into small, serious flakes
whipping sideways, piling fast. With a *Watch out,*

a snowball trailing white surprises her shoulder.
He laughs when her snowball finds its mark. Next,
he places her on their children's rickety Flexible
Flyer. They slide again and again down street's

slight hill—he pushing, she laughing—until snow's
sting brings them back. Inside, floor pillows pile—
they don't worry how he'll get her up. His gloved
hands set rough logs on open flame.

Drowsy from cold tempered into warmth, he
touches her hair, her cheek, cradles her upon
pillows and into her neck, murmurs, *Listen
to the wood burn.*

What He Needs to Hear

At home near their river,
she admires his ravishing
Valentine roses whose
intense swirl reveals
their deep interiors.
Expansive, he heaps
blessings on her,
whose simple homemade
card (the only kind he'll
accept) poetically states
what he needs to hear—
he gives her life and happiness—
and the shimmering red
of his Valentine's roses
match the depth of her
love for him.

That night, they sit on the glassed-in
sun porch, the complacent moon
perched in the late winter sky
above the neighborhood as if
to honor this love that she knows
is as real as this full moon's light
and its uncomplicated trajectory
on their yard white with new snow.

The Bird-Loud Day

The Delaware river's ice is done up in frozen
waves that crumple against the riverbank.

Scythe of heaving cold halts the river's flow
except for the blue corner of open water

where the current surfaces in the bottom left
of his photograph. It augurs spring—when

snowmelt will fill the channel and river's white-
caps will fling light onto burgeoning switchgrass.

Then, the bird-loud day will lack for nothing.

Anticipating the Sundial

~April 2020

He lifts her onto the bench under the Japanese maple, places
    a pillow behind her back, arranges a blanket over her legs,

kisses her, returns to the many-windowed house to prepare dinner.
    Eyes closed, she forgives her body its betrayals, doesn't

forgive the country's lack of preparedness for the latest
    devastation. Now in studded spring, this deadly virus

weighs heavy. She propels that worry into a still knot
    of the nearest oak and listens to neighbor's children play

tag on this blue bonnet of a Tuesday. No open schools, no toy stores
    or Disney, nor movies, nor swimming pools, while police

tape drapes boundaries of playgrounds, and locked gates guard
    parks. Shout-yellow tulips foretell spring's merry-making,

bird noise beats the air with *chip-chips,* whistles, trills. Today
    she must be content with listening to a rush of wings that

quiets the clamor of nestlings. How simple yet astounding to feed
    one's brood into quietness. The same with her own, whom

she fed in a chair under a tree on a day much like this one. No child
    is afflicted with what cripples their mother, nor has the deadly

virus stopped for them. She praises this fine-tuned day, anticipates
    the sundial marking light's last, red flare.

Tornado Watch

~ May 2020

There's a tornado watch today. Red and Japanese maples swing
    their black-with-rain branches over spring-green grass.
He awakens from his daily nap; she huddles away from storm's

sky as lightening seeks the ground. TV loudly beeps its tornado
    alert every five minutes until she turns it off, giving the two
of them over to wind and fate. There is this virus to worry

about now. Their current illnesses bring isolation—but the fear
    of catching this virus ratchets that up to seeing no one,
traveling nowhere. Who desires a life suddenly snapped shut?

They study their home's art as if visiting a museum and when storm
    clouds trail filaments of themselves toward the Delaware
wringing out over New Jersey lakes, the pine barrens, and then the ocean,

the sky clears. He pushes her wheelchair to tour their yard as if it
    were a park. Watchful, he scans their grass for dropped twigs,
branches. Hopeful, she searches for sunlight in its depths. Late spring

growth of purple weigela, red knockout roses, and snowdrop hydrangea's
    vigorous green and startling white assert the cycle. When brush-
topped wild grasses bend as one with every slight breeze, they proclaim
    that life thrives despite the grim number of lives taken.

They Need to Dream Here

From an impossible

    distance, sun

lights

    a path that cries

pleasure. One gold-veined

    lily

        awaits—a single

            thing,
humbling the dark.

    They need to dream here—

where disease can't

    send tentacles

to hijack nerve

        sheaths,

where they, thrilled,   find

    a place where disease can't reach,

        where the directionless

path leads home, where they

    awaken before

        the chasm-fall.

What Rises?

River water rises and rushes banks,
flattens thick grass, drowns the lowland
to please the Blue Heron with huge wing-

span rising, and Belted Kingfisher dropping
hard to high water, then triumphant, rising with
prey. Fast water foams over a tumble of rock

on the Jersey side where mist rises, a breath
beneath the bridge. Further up the bank,
saplings flourish their pale-green leaves,

and switchgrass rises yellow above the fast-
moving spring flood. What rises within the two
of them? Pulse full-throated, desiring hands' touch.

The Open Window

Morning's intense light brings a whirlpool
of desperation whose edges begin to swallow
her. *Lift your arms, grab my hands and you'll
rise out of it,* he says.

She does—his warm hands are almost as thin
as hers. Are they at the lake? An indigo bunting's
high-pitched call—*sweet sweet, chip chip*—
navigates the open window near the Delaware.

She's Radiant

This coming summer's horizon
will be very high around the opal

moon. She'll have long days to find
solace for what she must endure:

the work to straighten crooked limbs,
the IV medicine perhaps more poison

than miracle. For all this, her artist
could cover canvas with cadmium

yellow, manganese blue, Venetian
red, fold hints of cerulean and earth

brown, layer sea green and coral
rose until they shimmer and become

a painting of his woman as she was
and still is. She's on a porch swing—

the wooden one her grandfather made
sixty years ago—back straight, ankles

crossed, peach sundress bares her
shoulders. You can almost hear

the swing's slight creak, sense the way
her skin cools, see her wide smile

moving among riotous flowers massed
upon the banks of their river.

As if Surprised I Even Asked

She asked: "Would you
    (Handsome man climbing
    the basement stairs
    psychedelic poster
    in hand, purple
    headband askew
    from sifting
    through the 60's,
    exclaiming, "I found it!")

"have married
    (Sacred vow taken
    in light's leisure
    so that in difficult
    dark we can slow
    our breaths,
    determine if we
    can manage,
    endure, survive
    life's thorns.)

"me
    (Once whole, now not—
    a perfect example of a bet
    gone bad, of a love
    that could have soured
    like good, cold milk
    forgotten on the counter
    so that it's beyond
    buttermilk, beyond redemption.)

"then
      (*Riverside: under*
      Maxfield Parrish
      sky we lean toward
      river-blue pulsing,
      longing, life-brimming,
      rolling south to the deep
      ocean—both waters
      impervious
      to our intentions.)

"If you knew
      (recognized,
      perceived,
      discerned,
      realized,   ,
      fathomed)

"what you know
now?"
      (Travel truncated,
      leg brace follows
      us everywhere,
      no waltzing,
      no woodsy scent
      on our skin after
      a day's hike, no
      swimming in our
      New Hampshire lake—
      not a whit
      of any of those—.)

My chin cupped, raised
in your hand so eyes
can meet—

"Why, yes,"
you reply—
      (as if surprised
      I even asked).

Buttercup Light Shines Yellow

The mad-orange flare sinks later and later
toward the longest day of the year.
In their garden, their *Lucknow*, he pushes
her wheelchair—the unexpected five-petal
shimmer of buttercups spirals into view.
How did this yellow river over-spread
their entire side yard all the way to the back
fence? She watches him kneel, focus
his camera onto one yellow beauty.
What else is there?

To Die Just That Much

~ Wislawa Szymborska

Seduction and submission
sweep away her imagined dark
and its secrets.

Their attraction is selective after all.

They die just that much—treasure the hot,
brazen sun behind closed curtains that flutter
and shimmer like neon-blue dragonflies

above sweet green heat in long July—
where anything can happen
and does—

They Name Each Day Lucknow

Sunlight chisels its way over backyard's stand
of balsam fir, then releases sweet alyssum's white

scent. Heavenly Blue morning glories unravel
with heat's touch and blazing strawberries flood

the garden beyond narcissus that nestles among
scattered bricks. Aware of exquisite moments,

they name each day *Lucknow.* Every rain-full
evening, switchgrass battles washout. Each blade
stands guard.

Isn't That Enough?

They know the deck is stacked
against them, that joy easily shatters.
What if life relishes their woe?
What if that's the rule? If so,

they'll play the game with spirit,
never allow their imaginations to falter
and bend as far as they are able
with calamity. Isn't that enough?

For Love to Be Had

~ while listening to Mahler's
Symphony No. 2, *Resurrection*

But my love—we will not
find love in fear and dark-

ness but by stepping into
sunlight near our river

spreading wide and shallow
by the crossing. We reach

for cascading silver-blue
switchgrass—we touch

backs of hands, stroke
the edge of fingertips

sensitive beyond all reason,
feather heart's line.

There will be time for lifting
hands to yearning mouths,

for palms to be caressed,
for breasts to be cupped,

for muscles to be measured,
for love to be had—there

will be time for that.
There will be time.

Notes

Title of collection: *Switchgrass*. **The word also appears in many poems in the manuscript.**

Thundercloud	Cloud Nine	Dallas Blue

"Switchgrass (Panicum virgatum) is a perennial, warm season grass native to most of the eastern United States. It is drought and salt tolerant, needs little to no fertilizer and does well in shallow, wet soils. Deep, fibrous root systems to six feet improve soil and water quality by absorbing nutrients and sequestering carbon dioxide. This tall (up to 8 feet) bunch grass benefits wildlife, offering optimal nesting and cover. Switchgrass is a particularly beneficial flood season grass and is a year-round wild grass whose colors vary with the season."

https://www.ernstseed.com/wp-content/uploads/2017/01/Switchgrass-for-Riparian-Buffers.pdf
https://hoffmannursery.com/plants/details/panicum-virgatum-thundercloud-pp20665
https://hoffmannursery.com/plants/details/panicum-virgatum-cloud-nine
https://hoffmannursery.com/plants/details/panicum-virgatum-dallas-blues

40

Page 1 "Summertime Embraces Our Ten-Year-Old Selves"
Line 5: "discern time's wrinkle"
> Influenced by her title, *A Wrinkle in Time,* 1962, by
> American author, **Madeleine L'Engle (1918-2007)**

Page 1 "Summertime Embraces Our Ten-Year-Old Selves"
Line 14 *"Olly, olly, oxen free"*

"'**Olly, olly oxen free**' is a catchphrase or truce term used in children's games to indicate that players who are hiding can come out into the open without losing the game; that, or, alternatively, that the game is entirely over. The *Dictionary of American Regional English* says the phrase may be derived from *all ye, all ye outs in free*, or who are out may come in without penalty. Others speculate the phrase may be a corruption of a hypothetical and ungrammatical German phrase *alle, alle, auch sind frei* (all, all, also are free.") https://en.wikipedia.org/wiki/olly

Page 4 "Still"
Line 4 "**MS**" is an abbreviation for Multiple Sclerosis. "**Multiple Sclerosis** is an unpredictable autoimmune disease of the central nervous system that disrupts the flow of information within the brain and between the brain and muscles. For unknown reasons, **MS** causes the body's immune system to attack the fatty coating (myelin) of nerves in the brain and spinal cord. Symptoms include major muscle weakness (often in the hands, arms, back, and legs), tingling and burning and difficulties with vision. Scientists believe that a combination of environmental and genetic factors contribute to the risk of developing **MS.** There is no cure, although disease modifying drugs can lesson symptoms. Most people with **MS** are diagnosed between the ages of 20 and 50 and it occurs most commonly in women. **Multiple Sclerosis** affects some 400,000 Americans, and 2.5 million people worldwide." https://www.nationalmssociety.org

Line 5 "amyloidosis"
"**Amyloidosis** (am-uh-loi-DO-sis) is a rare disease that occurs when an abnormal protein, called *amyloid,* builds up in organs such as the heart, kidneys, liver, spleen, the nervous system, and digestive tract. It may be treated with disease modifying drugs and infusions of drugs that help the immune system. Some varieties of **amyloidosis** may lead to life-threatening organ failure. Most people diagnosed with **amyloidosis** are between ages 60 and 70, although earlier onset occurs. **Amyloidosis** occurs more commonly in men. Classified as a rare disease by the U.S. government, this means that it is estimated that all the types of **Amyloidosis** combined affect less than 200,000 people in the U.S. population.

https://www.mayoclinic.org/d.seases-conditions/amyloidosis/symptoms-causes/syc-20353178?_ga=

https://amyloidosis.org/facts/#:~:text=It%20is%20also%20referred%20to%20as%20an%20"orphan",As%20research%20continues%2C%20this%20rare%20classification%20may%20change.

Page 7 "Shaman ~ *after Octavio Paz*" Lines 14-21

> Visualize rebirth—between
> > what is seen
> and what is felt,
> > between what is felt
> and what is surmised,
> > between what
> is surmised and what is / known.

Lines by Mexican author, Octavio Paz (1914-1998),
from his poem, "Between What I See and What I Say":

> "Between what I see and what I say,
> Between what I say and what I feel.
> Between what I say and what I keep silent.
> Between what I keep silent and what I dream,
> Between what I dream and what I forget"

Paz, Octavio. "Between What I See and What I Say." <u>A Tree Within</u>. Translated by Eliot Weinberger. New York: New Directions. p. 4. lines 1-4.

Page 10 "Before Summer Sun Owns the Lake"
Line 20 "and waxy lilies that float like golden Fiestaware."

"Fiesta is a line of ceramic glazed dinnerware manufactured and marketed by the Fiesta Tableware Company of Newell, West Virginia since its introduction in 1936 with a hiatus from 1973 to 1985. Fiesta is noted for its Art Deco styling and its range of often bold, solid colors.

The company was known as the Homer Laughlin China Company (HLCC) until 2020, when it sold its food service divisions, along with the *Homer Laughlin* name, to Steelite, a British tableware manufacturer. HLCC in turn rebranded itself as the **Fiesta Tableware Company,** retaining its retail division, prominent Fiesta line, factories and headquarters in Newell, West Virginia.

According to the Smithsonian Institution Press, Fiesta's appeal lies in its colors, design, and affordability. In 2002, *The New York Times* called Fiesta «the most collected brand of china in the United States."

Fiesta was introduced at the annual Pottery and Glass Exhibit in Pittsburgh, Pennsylvania in January 1936. It was not the first solid color dinnerware in the US; smaller companies had been producing dinnerware, vases, and garden pottery sets, in solid color glazes for the better part of a decade by the time Fiesta was introduced to the market. However, Fiesta was the first widely mass-promoted and marketed solid-color dinnerware in the United States."

FIESTAWARE COSTAL COLORS 20 pc. SET DINNERWARE

FIESTAWRE BRIGHT COLORS 20 pc. DINNERWARE

. https://www.katom.com/learning-center/fiestaware-colorful history.html?CID=CJ&utm_source=cj&utm_medium=affiliate&utm_campaign=affiliate&cjevent=05c14d3b61c111ed81cc008c0a82b838 https://www.kohls.com/product/prd-2623492/fiesta-20-pc-place-setting.jsp?prdPV=1

Page 11, Title "In Every Life, Both." The line also appears in line 8 in the poem.

From:
Glück, Louise. "Presque Isle." <u>The Wild Iris</u>. York: Harper Collins, 1993. p. 43. line 1

Page 12 Title, *Lucknow*. The word also appears in other poems.
"'Lucknow' is the name of a mansion built in 1914 in Moultonborough, NH, by business tycoon Tom Plant and his wife, Oliva. The mansion—an architectural gem in the Arts and Crafts style—sits near a volcanic caldera of

the Ossipee Range, to the north of Lake Winnipesaukee. The original estate included over 6,500 acres of mountain forest. Today, Lucknow, known as *Castle in the Clouds,* is a popular tourist destination." http://lucknow.com/tomplantlucknow.htm

Page 16: Title, "Mooncake Festival"
"The Asian Mid-Autumn Festival is celebrated on the 15th day of the 8th lunar month, which is always in the middle of the autumn season in China. On the night of the **Mooncake Festival,** families place a table outside under the full harvest moon with mooncakes (round or square decorated stuffed pastries), fruits, and candles as sacrifices; they pray for good fortune. Families also light lanterns, sending them aloft to worship the moon and ancestors, hoping to bring good fortune to memorialize the Mid-Autumn night." https://www.travelchinaguide.com/essential/holidays/mid-autumn.html.

Page 19 "I Can Say Now That Things Are Not What They Seem."

Dr. CHRIS BURSK'S COMMENTS ON MARIE KANE'S POEM,
"I Can Say Now That Things Are Not What They Seem" --After Mark Strand, "Velocity Meadows"

From Bursk's essay on poetry and grief. (see bibliography below)

"This need to determine the terms of battle seems part of our evolutionary inheritance. Language, as poetry makes very clear, is not simply an instrument of communication, not even of self-expression, it is the way humans assert their right – however problematic –to define the world and thus to assert their dignity. Marie Kane, former poetry editor of *Pentimento*, a magazine whose title suggests its mission "to see beyond the surface" in celebrating the work of the disability community, offers in her poem an elegy for part of herself that life has conspired to begin depriving her. Once again, we find an instance of a poet's – no, a poem's – greed: to have more than just the experience itself: to have choice layered over choice, the poem doing what poetry does so well, sifting and revising. Revision itself is an exercise in greed. In the rest of our lives how often are we able to take back what we said and then change it till it's what we had wanted to say. In poetry we get to look and then look again – and at some distance."

"Strand's "Velocity Meadows," to which Marie Kane's poem refers contains the lines

> " 'I can say now that nothing was possible
> But leaving the house and standing in front of it, staring
> As long as I could into the valley. I knew that a train,
>
> Trailing a scarf of smoke, would arrive, that soon it would rain.
> A frieze of clouds lowered a shadow over the town,
> And a driving wind flattened the meadows' "

"The velocity of Strand's poem propels us past "I can say now that nothing was possible" and its fatalism and carries us to an implicit faith in observation and the transcendent gift that evolution offered us when it allowed us modifiers and metaphors: *a scarf of smoke, a frieze of clouds*. We find a similar shift in Kane's poem, from quad to *snow-tinged trees*. Just as with Strand, Kane is not merely *revisiting* a moment from the past but *revising* it. That new quad cane captures the tension of the poem; it is an instrument that reminds her of her increasing need for such an apparatus, but also allows mobility. And it also infers the mobility of language, for words in a poem rarely stay still. The line "I feel December's cold flicker like a tossed mane" calls to mind Strand's own metaphor of the train trailing its scarf of smoke. The mind did not just develop the capacity for metaphor, but a greed for it. And the mobility promises."

46

Bursk, Chris. *We Chew and Swallow: Grief, Language, and Dignity, Evolution's Extravagant Gifts.* **Essay. Poetry Workshop, Bucks County Community College, Newtown, PA. May 19, 2021.**

Reprinted with permission of the Bursk family and Chris Bursk's Literary Executor, Lorraine Henri Lins.

Page 21 "Their New Year"
Line 1 "Winter wind raises his blue and orange Delta." Delta kite:

"**Deltas** fly on the wind rather than against it. Their semi-flexible construction lets them fly in a wide range of winds, shifting and swooping with bird-like grace at each change in the wind. Adding tails stabilizes a Delta in high winds. They adopt an extremely high angle of flight and stay aloft better in uncertain winds than any other kind of kite."
https://intothewind.com/kites/delta-kites.html

Page 26 "Anticipating the Sundial"

Lines 18, 19 "nor has the deadly / virus stopped for them."
Influenced by American poet Emily Dickinson (1830-1882) Poem #479, circa 1863.
"Because I could not stop for Death—
He kindly stopped for me—"

Dickinson, Emily. "Because I Could Not Stop for Death." <u>The Poems of Emily *Dickinson*</u>. Ed. R.W. Franklin. Cambridge: Harvard University Press, 1999. p. 102. lines 1, 2.

Page 35, TITLE "To Die Just That Much" from:

Szymborska, Wislawa. "I'm Working on the World." <u>Poems New and Collected</u>. Translated from the Polish by Clare Cavanagh and Stanislaw Baranczak. New York: Harcourt, Inc., 1998. p. 3. lines 52 and 53.

Marie Kane Biography

Marie Kane is a lifelong writer. She credits her love of books and the written word to her mom, Jean Reddington, and to her English teachers, especially Paul Bradican of Dunmore High School, Dunmore Pa. She attended Bloomsburg University (PA) where she earned a BS degree in Secondary English Education and received a MS degree in English Education and Creative Writing from Arcadia University (PA) in 1995. She attended a Writing Seminar with Dana Gioia at Westchester University (PA) in 1992, and a Creative Writing Graduate Program at the University of New Hampshire in 1996.

Kane taught English and Creative Writing, grades10-12, in the Central Bucks School District (PA) for twenty-eight years, retiring in 2007.

She has been a featured reader at the New Jersey State Museum, James A. Michener Art Museum, the International House in Philadelphia, Musehouse in Philadelphia, Bucks County Community College, and at many bookstores, colleges, and libraries.

Kane is honored to be the 2006 Bucks County (PA) Poet Laureate.

Her poems have been anthologized in two Inglis House anthologies, the New Hampshire Poetry society's *The Poet's Touchstone (2008),* the *Delaware Valley Poets Anthology* (2009), the Bucks County Poets Laureate anthology, *Making Our Own Light* (2013), Valerie Fox and Lynn Levin's anthology, *Poems for the Writing: Prompts for Poets (2013 and 2019), and The Liberal Media Made Me Do It* (2014), poetic responses to NPR and PBS stories, edited by Robbie Nester, et al. Five of her poems were chosen for publication in *Touching MS*, an anthology edited by Jennifer Evans. Kane was chosen as the featured poet for the *Schuylkill Valley Journal* for the spring/summer issue of 2020.

The German author, Claudia Vesterby, chose her poem, "Radio Interview," to translate into German in the December 2012 issue of *Wordgathering*. Her work on the Greek goddess Persephone can be seen in two anthologies published by Bibliotheca Alexandrina (2014), editor Rebecca Buchanan: *Eternal Haunted Summer, Potnia,* and *Seasons of Grace: A Devotional in Honor of the Muses, the Charites, and the Horae.*

For several years, Kane was a final juror for the Montgomery County (PA) High School Poetry Contest, she is now a board member and judge for The Bucks County Main Street Voices poetry contest, student, and adult, and for the last fifteen years, has been the final judge for the international scholastic Sarah Mook poetry contest, grades K-12.

In June of 2012, Big Table Publishing of Newton, MA, launched her chapbook, *Survivors in the Garden,* which was used as a classroom text at Bucks County Community College by Dr. Christopher Bursk. The publisher, Robin Stratton, nominated the whole collection for a Pushcart Prize. Kane was diagnosed with multiple sclerosis in 1991, and with secondary progressive MS in 2005. Much of her work directly addresses her life with this disease, as the poems in *Survivors in the Garden* do. She also incorporates topics of nature and her family in her poetry.

She has published a full-length volume of poetry, *Beauty, You Drive a Hard Bargain* (Kelsay Books, 2017), and self-published a chapbook, *Persephone's Truth,* (2018) which includes her husband, Stephen Millner's, art.

She was the Poetry Editor for *Pentimento* magazine from 2013-2016; the magazine was devoted to publishing poetry, essays, fiction, creative non-fiction, art, and photography centering on people with disabilities and those who care for them. It sadly closed when the managing editor could no longer produce the magazine.

Marie Kane lives in Yardley, PA, with her husband, a photographer, painter, mixed media and assemblage artist, and their rescue cats Casey Jones and Emma Peel. They have five children between them and four boisterous grandsons. See more at www.mariekanepoetry.com.

Printed in the United States
by Baker & Taylor Publisher Services